Selected Poems 1940—1982

also by Norman Nicholson

A Local Habitation
Sea to the West

Selected Poems 1940—1982

Norman Nicholson

faber and faber

This selection first published in 1982
by Faber and Faber Limited
3 Queen Square London WC1N 3AU
Printed in Great Britain by
Latimer Trend & Company Ltd, Plymouth

British Library Cataloguing in Publication Data

Nicholson, Norman
   Selected poems, 1940–1982.
   I.   Title
   821.'912   PR6027.I/

   ISBN 0-571-11949-2
   ISBN 0-571-11950-6 Pbk

To YVONNE
with love as always

Contents

FIVE RIVERS (1944)

To the River Duddon

I wonder, Duddon, if you still remember
An oldish man with a nose like a pony's nose,
Broad bones, legs long and lean but strong enough
To carry him over Hard Knott at seventy years of age.
He came to you first as a boy with a fishing-rod
And a hunk of Ann Tyson's bread and cheese in his pocket,
Walking from Hawkshead across Walna Scar;
Then as a middle-aged Rydal landlord,
With a doting sister and a government sinecure,
Who left his verses gummed to your rocks like lichen,
The dry and yellow edges of a once-green spring.
He made a guide-book for you, from your source
There where you bubble through the moss on Wrynose
(Among the ribs of bald and bony fells
With screes scratched in the turf like grey scabs),
And twist and slither under humpbacked bridges—
Built like a child's house from odds and ends
Of stones that lie about the mountain side—
Past Cockley Beck Farm and on to Birk's Bridge,
Where the rocks stride about like legs in armour,
And the steel birches buckle and bounce in the wind
With a crinkle of silver foil in the crisp of the leaves;
On then to Seathwaite, where like a steam-navvy
You shovel and slash your way through the gorge
By Wallabarrow Crag, broader now
From becks that flow out of black upland tarns
Or ooze through golden saxifrage and the roots of rowans;
Next Ulpha, where a stone dropped from the bridge
Swims like a tadpole down thirty feet of water
Between steep skirting-boards of rock; and thence
You dribble into lower Dunnerdale
Through wet woods and wood-soil and woodland flowers,
Tutson, the St John's-wort with a single yellow bead,
Marsh marigold, creeping jenny and daffodils;
Here from hazel islands in the late spring

The catkins fall and ride along the stream
Like little yellow weasels, and the soil is loosed
From bulbs of the white lily that smells of garlic,
And dippers rock up and down on rubber legs,
And long-tailed tits are flung through the air like darts;
By Foxfield now you taste the salt in your mouth,
And thrift mingles with the turf, and the heron stands
Watching the wagtails. Wordsworth wrote:
'Remote from every taint of sordid industry'.
But you and I know better, Duddon.
For I, who've lived for nearly thirty years
Upon your shore, have seen the slagbanks slant
Like screes into the sand, and watched the tide
Purple with ore back up the muddy gullies,
And wiped the sinter dust from the farmyard damsons.
A hundred years of floods and rain and wind
Have washed your rocks clear of his words again,
Many of them half-forgotten, brimming the Irish Sea,
But that which Wordsworth knew, even the old man
When poetry had failed like desire, was something
I have yet to learn, and you, Duddon,
Have learned and re-learned to forget and forget again.
Not the radical, the poet and heretic,
To whom the water-forces shouted and the fells
Were like a blackboard for the scrawls of God,
But the old man, inarticulate and humble,
Knew that eternity flows in a mountain beck—
The long cord of the water, the shepherd's numerals
That run upstream, through the singing decades of dialect.
He knew, beneath mutation of year and season,
Flood and drought, frost and fire and thunder,
The blossom on the rowan and the reddening of the berries,
There stands the base and root of the living rock,
Thirty thousand feet of solid Cumberland.

Cleator Moor

From one shaft at Cleator Moor
They mined for coal and iron ore.
This harvest below ground could show
Black and red currants on one tree.

In furnaces they burnt the coal,
The ore was smelted into steel,
And railway lines from end to end
Corseted the bulging land.

Pylons sprouted on the fells,
Stakes were driven in like nails,
And the ploughed fields of Devonshire
Were sliced with the steel of Cleator Moor.

The land waxed fat and greedy too,
It would not share the fruits it grew,
And coal and ore, as sloe and plum,
Lay black and red for jamming time.

The pylons rusted on the fells,
The gutters leaked beside the walls,
And women searched the ebb-tide tracks
For knobs of coal or broken sticks.

But now the pits are wick with men,
Digging as dogs dig for a bone:
For food and life *we* dig the earth—
In Cleator Moor they dig for death.

Every wagon of cold coal
Is fire to drive a turbine wheel;
Every knuckle of soft ore
A bullet in a soldier's ear.

The miner at the rockface stands,
With his segged and bleeding hands
Heaps on his head the fiery coal,
And feels the iron in his soul.

ROCK FACE (1948)

St Luke's Summer

The low sun leans across the slanting field,
And every blade of grass is striped with shine
And casts its shadow on the blade behind,
And dandelion clocks are held
Like small balloons of light above the ground.

Beside the trellis of the bowling green
The poppy shakes its pepper-box of seed;
Groundsel feathers flutter down;
Roses exhausted by the thrust of summer
Lose grip and fall; the wire is twined with weed.

The soul, too, has its brown October days—
The fancy run to seed and dry as stone,
Rags and wisps of words blown through the mind;
And yet, while dead leaves clog the eyes,
Never-predicted poetry is sown.

Thomas Gray in Patterdale

I hold Helvellyn in my fingers, here
Ringed in the glass.* The clouds are still as paint,
And gills like tucks along the four-inch fells
Slant into neat diagonals. The lake
Is bright as sixpence; and if the wind
Bend back the bracken, it is but as hands
Rub shadows into plush against the pile.
There's not a breath of word or air or water
To blur the picture at the mirror's mouth.
But outside the glass
The breeze moves like a man; October trees
Scatter charred manuscripts; the sun
Includes me in its practice—I become
Part of a landscape that I cannot view,
And under the numbers of the wind I hear
Melodramatic crags and frantic thorns
Whispering simple names I almost know.
What if I listen? What if I learn?
What if I break the glass and turn
And face the objective lake and see
The wide-eyed stranger sky-line look at me?

* i.e. a Claude-glass—a small convex mirror in which it was possible to see
the landscape whole and in perspective.

THE POT GERANIUM (1954)

On Duddon Marsh

This is the shore, the line dividing
The dry land from the waters, Europe
From the Atlantic; this is the mark
That God laid down on the third day.
Twice a year the high tide sliding,
Unwrapping like a roll of oil-cloth, reaches
The curb of the mud, leaving a dark
Swipe of grease, a scaled-out hay

Of wrack and grass and gutterweed. Then
For full three hundred tides the bare
Turf is unwatered except for rain;
Blown wool is dry as baccy; tins
Glint in the sedge with not a sight of man
For two miles round to drop them there.
But once in spring and once again
In autumn, here's where the sea begins.

From a Boat at Coniston

I look into the lake (the lacquered water
Black with the sunset), watching my own face.
Tiny red-ribbed fishes swim
In and out of the nostrils, long-tongued weeds
Lick at the light that oozes down from the surface,
And bubbles rise from the eyes like aerated
Tears shed there in the element of mirrors.
My sight lengthens its focus; sees the sky
Laid level upon the glass, the loud
World of the wind and the map-making clouds and history
Squinting over the rim of the fell. The wind
Lets on the water, paddling like a duck,
And face and cloud are grimaced out
In inch-deep wrinkles of the moving waves.
A blackbird clatters; alder leaves
Make mooring buoys for the water beetles.
I wait for the wind to drop, against hope
Hoping, and against the weather, yet to see
The water empty, the water full of itself,
Free of the sky and the cloud and free of me.

Weather Ear

Lying in bed in the dark, I hear the bray
Of the furnace hooter rasping the slates, and say:
'The wind will be in the east, and frost on the nose, today.'

Or when, in the still, small, conscience hours, I hear
The market clock-bell clacking close to my ear:
'A north-west wind from the fell, and the sky-light swilled and
    clear.'

But now when the roofs are sulky as the dead,
With a snuffle and sniff in the gullies, a drip on the lead:
'No wind at all, and the street stone-deaf with a cold in the head.'

Millom Old Quarry

'They dug ten streets from that there hole,' he said,
'Hard on five hundred houses.' He nodded
Down the set of the quarry and spat in the water
Making a moorhen cock her head
As if a fish had leaped. 'Half the new town
'Came out of yonder—King Street, Queen Street, all
'The houses round the Green as far as the slagbank,
'And Market Street, too, from the Crown allotments
'Up to the Station Yard.'—'But Market Street's
'Brown freestone,' I said.—'Nobbut the facings;
'We called them the Khaki Houses in the Boer War,
'But they're Cumberland slate at the back.'

I thought of those streets still bearing their royal names
Like the coat-of-arms on a child's Jubilee Mug—
Nonconformist gables sanded with sun
Or branded with burning creeper; a smoke of lilac
Between the blue roofs of closet and coal-house:
So much that woman's blood gave sense and shape to
Hacked from this dynamited combe.
The rocks cracked to the pond, and hawthorns fell
In waterfalls of blossom. Shed petals
Patterned the scum like studs on the sole of a boot,
And stiff-legged sparrows skid down screes of gravel.

I saw the town's black generations
Packed in their caves of rock, as mussel or limpet
Washed by the tidal sky; then swept, shovelled
Back in the quarry again, a landslip of lintels
Blocking the gape of the tarn.
The quick turf pushed a green tarpaulin over
All that was mortal in five thousand lives.
Nor did it seem a paradox to one
Who held quarry and query, turf and town,
In the small box of a recording brain.

Rising Five

'I'm rising five', he said,
'Not four', and little coils of hair
Un-clicked themselves upon his head.
His spectacles, brimful of eyes to stare
At me and the meadow, reflected cones of light
Above his toffee-buckled cheeks. He'd been alive
Fifty-six months or perhaps a week more:

                                  not four,

But rising five.

Around him in the field the cells of spring
Bubbled and doubled; buds unbuttoned; shoot
And stem shook out the creases from their frills,
And every tree was swilled with green.
It was the season after blossoming,
Before the forming of the fruit:

                                  not May,

But rising June.

                 And in the sky
The dust dissected the tangential light:

                                  not day,

But rising night;

                 not now,

But rising soon.

The new buds push the old leaves from the bough.
We drop our youth behind us like a boy
Throwing away his toffee-wrappers. We never see the flower,
But only the fruit in the flower; never the fruit,
But only the rot in the fruit. We look for the marriage bed
In the baby's cradle, we look for the grave in the bed:

                                  not living,

But rising dead.

Five Minutes

'I'm having five minutes', he said,
Fitting the shelter of the cobble wall
Over his shoulders like a cape. His head
Was wrapped in a cap as green
As the lichened stone he sat on. The winter wind
Whined in the ashes like a saw,
And thorn and briar shook their red
Badges of hip and haw;
The fields were white with smoke of blowing lime;
Rusty iron brackets of sorrel stood
In grass grey as the whiskers round an old dog's nose.
'Just five minutes', he said;
And the next day I heard that he was dead,
Having five minutes to the end of time.

Gathering Sticks on Sunday

If the man in the moon,
Gazing at the waning earth, watches
How the frayed edge of the sunset catches
Thimbles and nodules of rock,
Hachuring distinct with threads of shadow
All that is hammered flat in the earth's brass noon;
And if he sees,
New in the level light, like pock-
marks on a face, dark craters
The size of acorn cups, or scars
Vast as his own dried oceans, then
He'll know that soon
The living world of men
Will take a lunar look, as dead as slag,
And moon and earth will stare at one another
Like the cold, yellow skulls of child and mother.

The Undiscovered Planet

Out on the furthest tether let it run
Its hundred-year-long orbit, cold
As solid mercury, old and dead
Before this world's fermenting bread
Had got a crust to cover it; landscape of lead
Whose purple voes and valleys are
Lit faintly by a sun
No nearer than a measurable star.

No man has seen it; the lensed eye
That pin-points week by week the same patch of sky
Records not even a blur across its pupil. Only
The errantry of Saturn, the wry
Retarding of Uranus, speak
Of the pull beyond the pattern:
The unknown is shown
Only by a bend in the known.

Green slated gables clasp the stem of the hill
In the lemony autumn sun; an acid wind
Dissolves the leaf stalks of back garden trees,
And chimneys with their fires unlit
Seem yet to puff a yellow smoke of poplars.
Freestone is brown as bark, and the model bakery
That once was a Primitive Methodist Chapel
Lifts its cornice against the sky.
And now, like a flight of racing pigeons
Slipped from their basket in the station yard,
A box kite rides the air, a square of calico,
Crimson as the cornets of the Royal Temperance Band
When they brass up the wind in marching. The kite
Strains and struggles on its leash, and unseen boys,
In chicken run or allotment or by the side
Of the old quarry full to the gullet with water,
Pay out on their string a rag of dream,
High as the Jubilee flagpole.
                    I turn from the window
(Letting the bobbins of autumn wind up the swallows)
And lie on my bed. The ceiling
Slopes over like a tent, and white walls
Wrap themselves round me, leaving only
A flap for the light to blow through. Thighs and spine
Are clamped to the mattress and looping springs
Twine round my chest and hold me. I feel the air
Move on my face like spiders, see the light
Slide across the plaster; but wind and sun
Are mine no longer, nor have I kite to claim them,
Or string to fish the clouds. But there on a shelf
In the warm corner of my dormer window
A pot geranium flies its bright balloon,
Nor can the festering hot-house of the tropics
Breed a tenser crimson; for this crock of soil,
Six inch deep by four across,

Contains the pattern, the prod and pulse of life,
Complete as the Nile or the Niger.
                    And what need therefore
To stretch for the straining kite?—for kite and flower
Bloom in my room for ever; the light that lifts them
Shines in my own eyes, and my body's warmth
Hatches their red in my veins. It is the Gulf Stream
That rains down the chimney, making the soot spit; it is the
    Trade Wind
That blows in the draught under the bedroom door.
My ways are circumscribed, confined as a limpet
To one small radius of rock; yet
I eat the equator, breathe the sky, and carry
The great white sun in the dirt of my finger nails.

A LOCAL HABITATION (1972)

The Whisperer

For twenty months I whispered,
        Spoke aloud
        Not one word,
Except when the doctor, checking my chest, said:
        'Say Ninety-nine',
        And, from the mine
Of my throat, hauling up my voice like a load of metal, I
        Said 'Ninety-nine.'
        From sixteen-
years-old to my eighteenth birthday I whispered clock
        And season round;
        Made no sound
More than the wind that entered without knocking
        Through the door
        That wasn't there
Or the slid-wide window that un-shuttered half the wall of my
        Shepherd's bothy
        Of a chalet.
In the hushed sanatorium night I coughed in whispers
        To stray cats
        And dogs that
Stalked in from the forest fogs to the warmth of my anthracite
          stove.
        Day after day
        My larynx lay
In dry dock until whispering seemed
        The normal way
        Of speaking: I
Was surprised at the surprise on the face of strangers
        Who wondered why
        I was so shy.
When I talked to next-bed neighbours, out-of-breath on the
        Gravel track,
        They whispered back

As if the practice were infectious. Garrulous as a budgie,
      I filled the air
      Of my square
Thermometered and Lysolled cage with the agitated
      Wheezes, squeaks
      And wind-leaks
Of my punctured Northumbrian pipes. And when the doctor
      asked me
      How I felt, 'I'm
      Feeling fine',
I whispered—my temperature down to thirty-seven,
      The sore grate
      Soothed from my throat,
And all the winds of Hampshire to ventilate my lungs.

Two winters went whispered away before I ventured
      Out of my cage,
      Over the hedge,
On to the chalky chines, the sparse, pony-trodden, adder-ridden
      Grass. Alone
      Among pine
Trunks I whispered comfortable sermons to
      Congregations
      Of worms. Patients
On exercise in copse or on common, sighting me
      At distance, gave
      Me a wave,
And I in reply blew a blast on my police-
      man's whistle,
      Meaning: 'Listen.
Wait! Come closer. I've something to tell.'
      But when tea-
      time brought me
To drawing-room and chatter, the thunder of shook cups,
      Crack of laughter,
      Stunned and baffled
Me. I bawled in whispers four-inch from the ear
      Of him or her
      Unheeded. Words,

Always unheard, failed even articulate me.
              Frantic, I'd rap
              Table or clap
Hands, crying: 'Listen, for God's sake listen!' And suddenly the
              room
              Fell silent,
              Waiting, and I
Words failing again, fell silent too.
                              The world moved
              Noisily on.
              My larynx soon
Was afloat again but my life still drifts in whispers.
              I shout out loud
              To no crowd,
Straining to be heard above its strangling murmur, but
              Look for one face
              Lit with the grace
Of listening, the undeadened brow that marks an undeafened
              Ear. I try
              To catch an eye;
Nod, nudge, wink, beckon, signal with clicked
              Fingers, roll
              Words to a ball
And toss them for the wind to play with. Life roars round me
              like
              A dynamo.
              I stump, stamp, blow
Whistle over and over, staring into the rowdy air, seeking
              You or you,
              Anyone who
Can lip-read the words of my whisper as clear as the clang of a
              bell,
              Can see me say:
              'Wait! Wait!
              Come closer;
              I've something to tell.'

The Black Guillemot

Midway between Fleswick and St Bees North Head,
The sun in the west,
All Galloway adrift on the horizon;
The sandstone red
As dogwood; sea-pink, sea campion and the sea itself
Flowering in clefts of the cliff—
And down on one shelf,
Dozen on dozen pressed side by side together,
White breast by breast,
Beaks to the rock and tails to the fish-stocked sea,
The guillemots rest

Restlessly. Now and then,
One shifts, clicks free of the cliff,
Wings whirling like an electric fan—
Silhouette dark from above, with under-belly gleaming
White as it banks at the turn—
Dives, scoops, skims the water,
Then, with all Cumberland to go at, homes
To the packed slum again,
The rock iced with droppings.

I swing my binoculars into the veer of the wind,
Sight, now, fifty yards from shore,
That rarer auk: all black,
But for two white patches where the wings join the back,
Alone like an off-course migrant
(Not a bird of his kind
Nesting to the south of him in England),
Yet self-subsistent as an Eskimo,
Taking the huff if so much as a feather
Lets on his pool and blow-hole
In the floating pack-ice of gulls.

But, turn the page of the weather,
Let the moon haul up the tides and the pressure-hose of spray
Swill down the lighthouse lantern—then,
When boats keep warm in harbour and bird-watchers in bed,
When the tumble-home of the North Head's rusty hull
Takes the full heave of the storm,
The hundred white and the one black flock
Back to the same rock.

Hodbarrow Flooded

Where once the bogies bounced along hummocking tracks,
A new lake spreads its edges.
Where quarried ledges were loaded with red-mould ore,
Old winding towers
Up-ended float on glass.
Where once the shafts struck down through yielding limestone,
Black coot and moorhen
Lay snail-wakes on the water.

At seventy fathom
My Uncle Jack was killed
With half a ton of haematite spilled on his back.
They wound him up to the light
Still gasping for air.

Not even the rats can gasp there now:
For, beneath the greening spoil of a town's life-time,
The sixty, seventy,
Ninety fathom levels
Are long pipes and throttles of unflowing water,
Stifled cavities,
Lungs of a drowned man.

On the Closing of Millom Ironworks

September 1968

Wandering by the heave of the town park, wondering
Which way the day will drift,
On the spur of a habit I turn to the feathered
Weathercock of the furnace chimneys.
                                    But no grey smoke-tail
Pointers the mood of the wind. The hum
And blare that for a hundred years
Drummed at the town's deaf ears
Now fills the air with the roar of its silence.
They'll need no more to swill the slag-dust off the windows;
The curtains will be cleaner
And the grass plots greener
Round the Old Folk's council flats. The tanged autumnal mist
Is filtered free of soot and sulphur,
And the wind blows in untainted.
But, morning after morning, there
They stand, by the churchyard gate,
Hands in pockets, shoulders to the slag,
The men whose fathers stood there back in '28,
When their sons were at school with me.
                                    The town
Rolls round the century's bleak orbit.
                                    Down
On the ebb-tide sands, the five-funnelled
Battleship of the furnace lies beached and rusting;
Run aground, not foundered;
Not a crack in her hull;
Lacking but a loan to float her off.
                                    The Market
Square is busy as the men file by
To sign on at the 'Brew'.* But not a face
Tilts upward, no one enquires of the sky.

The smoke prognosticates no how
Or why of any practical tomorrow.
For what does it matter if it rains all day?
And what's the good of knowing
Which way the wind is blowing
When whichever way it blows it's a cold wind now.

* The local term for 'Bureau'—i.e. Labour Exchange—widely used in the 1930s.

42

Windscale

The toadstool towers infest the shore:
Stink-horns that propagate and spore
    Wherever the wind blows.
Scafell looks down from the bracken band,
And sees hell in a grain of sand,
    And feels the canker itch between his toes.

This is a land where dirt is clean,
And poison pasture, quick and green,
    And storm sky, bright and bare;
Where sewers flow with milk, and meat
Is carved up for the fire to eat,
    And children suffocate in God's fresh air.

'The tune the old cow died of,'
My grandmother used to say
When my uncle played the flute.
She hadn't seen a cow for many a day,
Shut in by slate
Walls that bound her
To scullery and yard and soot-
blackened flowerpots of hart's-tongue fern.
She watched her fourteen sons grow up around her
In a back street,
Blocked at one end by crags of slag,
Barred at the other by the railway goods-yard gate.
The toot of the flute
Piped to a parish where never cow could earn
Her keep—acres of brick
With telegraph poles and chimneys reared up thick
As ricks in a harvest field.
My grandmother remembered
Another landscape where the cattle
Waded half-way to the knees
In swish of buttercup and yellow rattle,
And un-shorn, parasite-tormented sheep
Flopped down like grey bolsters in the shade of trees,
And the only sound
Was the whine of a hound
In the out-of-hunting-season summer,
Or the cheep of wide-beaked, new-hatched starlings,
Or the humdrum hum of the bees.   *Then*
A cow meant milk, meant cheese, meant money,
And when a cow died
With foot-and-mouth or wandered out on the marshes
And drowned at the high tide,
The children went without whatever their father had promised.
When she was a girl
There was nothing funny,

My grandmother said,
About the death of a cow,
And it isn't funny now
To millions hungrier even than she was then.
So when the babies cried,
One after each for over fourteen years,
Or the flute squeaked at her ears,
Or the council fire-alarm let off a scream
Like steam out of a kettle and the whole mad town
Seemed fit to blow its lid off—she could find
No words to ease her mind
Like those remembered from her childhood fears:
'The tune the old cow died of.'

'Have you been to London?'
My grandmother asked me.
                              'No.'—
China dogs on the mantelshelf,
Paper blinds at the window,
Three generations simmering on the bright black lead,
And a kettle filled to the neb,
Spilled over long ago.

I blew into the room, threw
My scholarship cap on the rack;
Wafted visitors up the flue
With the draught of my coming in—
Ready for Saturday's mint imperials,
Ready to read
The serial in *Titbits*, the evangelical
Tale in the parish magazine,
Under the green
Glare of the gas,
Under the stare of my grandmother's Queen.

My grandmother burnished her sleek steel hair—
Not a tooth in her jaw
Nor alphabet in her head,
Her spectacles lost before I was born,
Her lame leg stiff in the sofa corner,
Her wooden crutch at the steady:
'They shut doors after them
In London,' she said.

I crossed the hearth and thumped the door *to*;
Then turned to Saturday's stint,
My virtuosity of print
And grandmother's wonder:
Reading of throttler and curate,

Blood, hallelujahs and thunder,
While the generations boiled down to one
And the kettle burned dry
In a soon grandmotherless room;

Reading for forty years,
Till the print swirled out like a down-catch of soot
And the wind howled round
A world left cold and draughty,
Un-latched, un-done,
By all the little literate boys
Who hadn't been to London.

'It's mending worse,' he said,
Bending west his head,
Strands of anxiety ravelled like old rope,
Skitter of rain on the scorer's shed
His only hope.

Seven down for forty-five,
Catches like stings from a hive,
And every man on the boundary appealing—
An evening when it's bad to be alive,
And the swifts squealing.

Yet without boo or curse
He waits leg-break or hearse,
Obedient in each to law and letter—
Life and the weather mending worse,
Or worsening better.

Nicholson, Suddenly

From the BARROW EVENING MAIL, Thurs, 13th Feb., 1969

'NICHOLSON—(Suddenly) on February 11, Norman, aged
57 years, beloved husband of Mona Nicholson, and dear
father of Gerald, of 6 Atkinson Street, Haverigg, Millom.'

So Norman Nicholson is dead!
I saw him just three weeks ago
Standing outside a chemist's shop,
His smile alight, his cheeks aglow.
I'd never seen him looking finer:
'I can't complain at all,' he said,
'But for a touch of the old angina.'
Then hobbled in for his prescription.
Born in one town, we'd made our start,
Though not in any way related,
Two years and three streets apart,
Under one nominal description:
'Nicholson, Norman', entered, dated,
In registers of birth and school.
In 1925 we sat
At the same desk in the same class—
Me, chatty, natty, nervous, thin,
Quick for the turn of the teacher's chin;
Silent, shy and smiling, he,
And fleshed enough for two of me—
An unidentical near twin
Who never pushed his presence in
When he could keep it out.
                            For seven
Years after that each neither knew,
Nor cared much, where or even whether
The other lived. And then, together,
We nearly booked out berths to heaven:—
Like a church weathercock, *I* crew
A graveyard cough and went to bed
For fifteen months; *he* dropped a lead
Pipe on his foot and broke them both.

They wheeled him home to his young wife
Half-crippled for the rest of life.

In three decades or more since then
We met, perhaps, two years in ten
In shops or waiting for a bus;
Greeted each other without fuss,
Just: 'How do, Norman?'—Didn't matter
Which of us spoke—we said the same.
And now and then we'd stop to natter:
'How's the leg?' or 'How's the chest?'—
He a crock below the waist
And me a crock above it.
                              Blessed
Both with a certain home-bred gumption,
We stumped our way across the cobbles
Of half a life-time's bumps and roughness—
He short in step and me in wind,
Yet with a kind of wiry toughness.
Each rather sorry for the other,
We chose the road that suited best—
Neither inscribed the sky with flame;
Neither disgraced the other's name.
And now, perhaps, one day a year
The town will seem for half a minute
A place with one less person in it,
When I remember I'll not meet
My unlike double in the street.
Postmen will mix us up no more,
Taking my letters to his door,
For which I ought to raise a cheer.
But can I stir myself to thank
My lucky stars, when there's a blank
Where *his* stars were? For I'm left here,
Wearing his name as well as mine,
Finding the spare one doesn't fit,
And, though I'll make the best of it,
Sad that such things had to be—
But glad, still, that it wasn't me.

Great Day

'I gave him an—*err*,' my father said, meaning
Masonic handshake: holding his fingers
As if they still were sticky from the royal touch.
And I, at an upstairs window (the afternoon
Raining down on the Square, the Holborn Hill Brass Bandsmen
Blowing the water out of their tubas) watched
His Royal Highness conducted through the puddles
To my father's brotherly clasp.
                              Out in the wet,
Beside the broken billboards and the derelict joiner's yard,
Two hundred primary scholars soaked and cheered,
Unseeing and unseen.
                      At five o'clock that morning
We'd climbed the Jubilee Hill in the drizzling forelight
To view, in ninety-nine per cent eclipse, a sun
That never rose at all. The smoke from early fires
Seeped inconspicuously into the mist; the 5.30
Ironworks buzzer boomed out like a fog-horn. Click,
On the nick of the clock, the calculated dawn
Shied back on itself, birds knocked off shouting,
And the light went home to roost. Two minutes later
The twist of the globe turned up the dimmer
And day began again to try to begin.
                                     It rained,
On and off, for eleven hours, but I
Dry in my window-seat, the sun still in eclipse,
Squinted at the prince through candle-kippered glasses,
Too young to be disappointed, too old to cheer—
Universe and dynasty poised on the tip of one parish—
Eager at last, for *God Save the King* and tea
And my father's now royally contagious hand.

The Cock's Nest

The spring my father died—it was winter, really,
February fill-grave, but March was in
Before we felt the bruise of it and knew
How empty the rooms were—that spring
A wren flew to our yard, over Walter Willson's
Warehouse roof and the girls' school playground
From the old allotments that are now no more than a compost
For raising dockens and cats. It found a niche
Tucked behind the pipe of the bathroom outflow,
Caged in a wickerwork of creeper; then
Began to build:
Three times a minute, hour after hour,
Backward and forward to the backyard wall,
Nipping off neb-fulls of the soot-spored moss
Rooted between the bricks. In a few days
The nest was finished. They say the cock
Leases an option of sites and leaves the hen
To choose which nest she will. She didn't choose our yard.
And as March gambolled out, the fat King-Alfred sun
Blared down too early from its tinny trumpet
On new-dug potato-beds, the still bare creeper,
The cock's nest with never an egg in,
And my father dead.

The Seventeenth of the Name

When my grandmother in a carrier's cart, fording the mile and
a half wide
Ebb of the Duddon, saw the black marsh sprouting
      Furnace and shack,
      'Turn the horse back!'
She cried, but the tide had turned and the horse went on. My
land-bred grand-
father, harnessed farm hacks to works waggons, shifted grit
from the quarries,
      And laid down
      The road to the town
Before the town was there. My Uncle Bill,
Bundled in with the eggs and the luggage at fifteen months,
hatched out to be a blacksmith,
      Served his hour
      To horseless horse-power,
Forged shoes for machines and iron pokers, hooked
Like a butcher's skewer, for my grandmother's kitchen range.

      My Uncle Jack
      Played full-back
For the Northern Union and went in second wicket for the
First Eleven.
One August Monday he smacked a six clean into an excursion
train—
      'Hit it from here
      To Windermere',
My grandmother said. He broke his spine down the mine and
died below ground
(The family's prided loss on the iron front),
      Left, 'Not to Mourn',
      A daughter, born
After he died, and a widow who held to his memory fifty years.
My Uncle Tom was a cobbler: under a crack willow of leather
shavings

Tacked boot, nailed clog,
By the twitch of dog-
eared Co-operative gas-jets in the dark of the shoe shop where
My Uncle Jim was manager. He, best-loved uncle
And my father's friend,
In the end
Out-lived the lot: octogenarian, in a high, stiff collar, he walked
his silver-
banded cane down the half-day closings
Of a vast, life-lasting,
Somnambulist past.
My Uncle George married Jim's wife's sister and left with my
Uncle Fred
To be bosses' weighman and men's check-weighman in the
same Durham pit. Each
Bargained each black
Over half tons of slack,
And they went for a walk together every Sunday morning.
My Uncle Bob, a Tom-Thumb tailor, as my grandmother
told me,
Sat cross-legged all day
On a thimble; went to stay
With George, drove out on a motor-bike and rode back in a
hearse.
Arnold, the youngest, hung wall-paper; Harry was a waiter;
Richard took fits. Three
Died in infancy,
Un-christened and un-sistered. One other brother
Left me what an uncle couldn't:—a face, a place, a root
That drives down deep
As St George's steeple
Heaves up high.—The church was built in the year that he was
born.—
The name is painted out on the sun-blind of my father's shop,
But yellows yet
In files of *The Millom Gazette*,
And in minutes of the Musical Festival and the Chamber of
Trade;
And in lead letters on headstones by St George's mound

It now spells out
Its what-are-you-going-to-do-about-it
Memorandum. As once when a boy I see it scratched
On backstreet slates and schoolyard gates. Step on the
                                    gravel and the stones squeak out
'Nicholson, Nicholson.'
Whereupon
Grandmother, grandfather, father, seven known
And six clocked-out-before-me uncles stare
From their chimneyed heaven
On the seventeenth
Of the name, wondering through the holy smother where the
                                    family's got to.
And I, in their great-grand-childless streets, rake up for my reply
Damn all but hem
And haw about them.

SEA TO THE WEST (1981)

Scafell Pike

Look
Along the well
Of the street,
Between the gasworks and the neat
Sparrow-stepped gable
Of the Catholic chapel,
High
Above tilt and crook
Of the tumbledown
Roofs of the town—
Scafell Pike,
The tallest hill in England.

How small it seems,
So far away,
No more than a notch
On the plate-glass window of the sky!
Watch
A puff of kitchen smoke
Block out peak and pinnacle—
Rock-pie of volcanic lava
Half a mile thick
Scotched out
At the click of an eye.

Look again
In five hundred, a thousand or ten
Thousand years:
A ruin where
The chapel was; brown
Rubble and scrub and cinders where
The gasworks used to be;
No roofs, no town,
Maybe no men;
But yonder where a lather-rinse of cloud pours down

The spiked wall of the sky-line, see,
Scafell Pike
Still there.

Beck

Not the beck only,
Not just the water—
The stones flow also,
Slow
As continental drift,
As the growth of coral,
As the climb
Of a stalagmite.
Motionless to the eye,
Wide cataracts of rock
Pour off the fellside,
Throw up a spume
Of gravel and scree
To eddy and sink
In the blink of a lifetime.
The water abrades,
Erodes; dissolves
Limestones and chlorides;
Organizes its haulage—
Every drop loaded
With a millionth of a milligramme of fell.
The falling water
Hangs steady as stone;
But the solid rock
Is a whirlpool of commotion,
As the fluid strata
Crest the curl of time,
And top-heavy boulders
Tip over headlong,
An inch in a thousand years.
A Niagara of chock-stones,
Bucketing from the crags,
Spouts down the gullies.
Slate and sandstone
Flake and deliquesce,

And in a grey
Alluvial sweat
Ingleborough and Helvellyn
Waste daily away.
The pith of the pikes
Oozes to the marshes,
Slides along the sykes,
Trickles through ditch and dub,
Enters the endless
Chain of water,
The pull of earth's centre—
An irresistible momentum,
Never to be reversed,
Never to be halted,
Till the tallest fell
Runs level with the lowland,
And scree lies flat as shingle,
And every valley is exalted,
Every mountain and hill
Flows slow.

Sea to the West

When the sea's to the west
The evenings are one dazzle—
You can find no sign of water.
Sun upflows the horizon;
Waves of shine
Heave, crest, fracture,
Explode on the shore;
The wide day burns
In the incandescent mantle of the air.

Once, fifteen,
I would lean on handlebars,
Staring into the flare,
Blinded by looking,
Letting the gutterings and sykes of light
Flood into my skull.

Then, on the stroke of bedtime,
I'd turn to the town,
Cycle past purpling dykes
To a brown drizzle
Where black-scum shadows
Stagnated between backyard walls.
I pulled the warm dark over my head
Like an eiderdown.

Yet in that final stare when I
(Five times, perhaps, fifteen)
Creak protesting away—
The sea to the west,
The land darkening—
Let my eyes at the last be blinded
Not by the dark
But by dazzle.

Shingle

It surges down—
Slow underpull
Of heavy grey waves,
Meeting the sea's
Surge upwards.

Never a backflow, always
This crawl of a fall.
On the line of the swell
Each long crest crumbles
Into a sud of stone
Medallions and ovals,
Smooth as butterbeans;
But the shoulder of the wave
Is cumbered with cobbles
The size a stone-waller
Might pile into a barn.

At the bank's bottom step
The obtuse-angled
Thrust of the tide
Shovels the pebbles
Inwards and slant-wise,
For the surf to suck back again
The breadth of a winkle-shell
From where they were before.

A mounded migration
Of crab-backed stones,
Tide by tide, moves
Sideways along the shore.

But here at the highest
Rung of the rise—
A gull's stride under

The shivering overhang
Of sea-spurge and marram—
Only the wildest
Tides arrive
To dump sacks of boulders
On the shrivelled wrack,
Where the stones reside
A while on their circuit,
Inch by inch
Rolling round England.

Cloud on Black Combe

The air clarifies. Rain
Has clocked off for the day.

The wind scolds in from Sligo,
Ripping the calico-grey from a pale sky.
Black Combe holds tight
To its tuft of cloud, but over the three-legged island
All the west is shining.

An hour goes by,
And now the starched collars of the eastern pikes
Streak up into a rinse of blue. Every
Inland fell is glinting;
Black Combe alone still hides
Its bald, bleak forehead, balaclava'd out of sight.

Slick fingers of wind
Tease and fidget at wool-end and wisp,
Picking the mist to bits.
Strings and whiskers
Fray off from the cleft hill's
Bilberried brow, disintegrate, dissolve
Into blue liquidity—
Only a matter of time
Before the white is wholly worried away
And Black Combe starts to earn its name again.

But where, in the west, a tide
Of moist and clear-as-a-vacuum air is piling
High on the corried slopes, a light
Fret and haar of hazy whiteness
Sweats off the cold rock; in a cloudless sky
A cloud emulsifies,
Junkets on sill and dyke.
Wool-end and wisp materialize

Like ectoplasm, are twined
And crocheted to an off-white,
Over-the-lughole hug-me-tight;
And Black Combe's ram's-head, butting at the bright
Turfed and brackeny brine,
Gathers its own wool, plucks shadow out of shine.

What the wind blows away
The wind blows back again.

Nobbut God

First on
There was silence.
And God said:
'Let there be clatter.'

The wind, unclenching,
Runs its thumbs
Along dry bristles of Yorkshire Fog.

The mountain ousel
Oboes its one note.

After rain
Water lobelia
Drips like a tap
On the tarn's tight surface-tension.

But louder,
And every second nearer,
Like chain explosions
From furthest nebulae
Light-yearing across space:
The thudding of my own blood.

'It's nobbut me,'
Says God.

Glacier

Its hectares of white
Out of sight from below,
It gropes with one green paw
The rim of the rock-fall.
Each claw
A crunching of bottle-glass,
Opaque and raw,
Splinters as big as a cottage
Cracked between tongs:
A malevolent, rock-crystal
Precipitate of lava,
Corroded with acid,
Inch by inch erupting
From volcanoes of cold.

Slow
Paws creak downwards,
Annexing no
Extra acreage of stone—
For each hooked talon
Is pruned back and pared
By mid-June sun,
And a hundred sluicings
Ooze down the inclined plane
To a wizened, terminal
Half-cone of snow.

The ebb and flow
Of becks that live for a minute
Swishes bath-salt icebergs
Through a shingle moraine—
Where the dandy, grey-rust

Fieldfare rattles
Pebbles in its crop,
And the dwarf cornel
Blinks like a black-eyed buttercup
On the brink of the milk of melting.

Summer now
Out-spills the corrie
With a swill of willow,
But winter's overhang
Retreats not a centimetre—
No fractured knuckle, no
Refrigerated bone
Relinquishes grasp,
Lets slip a finger-hold
To the bland noon's seepage.

For behind black
Rock-terraces and tiers
Slumped winter waits—
For a tilt of earth's axis,
A stretching-out of the polar cold,
To restore the normal, to correct
The climate's misdirection,
Corroborate and order
Mean average temperature
For the last million years.

Cornthwaite

Cornthwaite, 'the clearing of the corn',
My mother's maiden-name—whose umpteenth great-grandfather,
Off-come from a northern voe, hacked thorn,
Oak-scrub and birch from rake and beck-bank
To sow his peck of oats, not much of a crop.
Lish as a wind-racked larch, he took his trod
Through landscape nameless still to him, until,
Remembering his own grandfather's talk
Of *tveit* and *dal* and *fjell*,
He scratched those words on the rocks,
Naming the Cymric cwms in a Norse tongue.
The land then named him back.
And here, a millennium later, my baptismal card
Clacks echoes of a clearing beneath cracked
Granite and black pines, where the migrant fieldfare breeds
And the ungregarious, one-flowered cloudberry
Is commoner than crowding bramble. Now,
In my own day's dale, under the slant
Scree of unstable time, I lop,
Chop and bill-hook at thickets and rankness of speech,
Straining to let light in, make space for a word,
To hack out once again my inherited thwaite
And sow my peck of poems, not much of a crop.

Weeds

Some people are flower lovers.
I'm a weed lover.

Weeds don't need planting in well-drained soil;
They don't ask for fertilizer or bits of rag to scare away birds.
They come without invitation;
And they don't take the hint when you want them to go.
Weeds are nobody's guests:
More like squatters.

Coltsfoot laying claim to every new-dug clump of clay;
Pearlwort scraping up a living between bricks from a ha'porth
    of mortar;
Dandelions you daren't pick or you know what will happen;
Sour docks that make a first-rate poultice for nettle-stings;
And flat-foot plantain in the back street, gathering more dust
    than the dustmen.

Even the names are a folk-song:
Fat hen, rat's tail, cat's ear, old men's baccy and Stinking Billy
Ring a prettier chime for me than honeysuckle or jasmine,
And Sweet Cicely smells cleaner than Sweet William though she's
    barred from the garden.

And they have their uses, weeds.
Think of the old, worked-out mines:
Quarries and tunnels, earth scorched and scruffy, torn-up
    railways, splintered sleepers,
And a whole Sahara of grit and smother and cinders.

But go in summer and where is all the clutter?
For a new town has risen of a thousand towers,
Every spiky belfry humming with a peal of bees.
Rosebay willow-herb:
Only a weed!

Flowers are for wrapping in cellophane to present as a bouquet;
Flowers are for prize arrangements in vases and silver tea-pots;
Flowers are for plaiting into funeral wreaths.
You can keep your flowers.
Give me weeds.

The Bloody Cranesbill

Every Sunday morning, when I was ten or twelve,
My father and I set off and called on my Uncle Jim
For the weekly fraternal walk. Five minutes' talk with my
    Auntie,
Then through the allotments, the playing-field, the lonning, out
To the links and warrens and foreshore of the already dying
    mine
That yet had thirty more years of dying to live through. No
    longer
The bustle and clang of my father's apprentice days—a thousand
Boots reddening the road at the end of the morning shift:
A Sabbath Day quiet now, no sound but the ricochet,
On the vast, glass, railway-station roof of sky, of the chuff and
    splutter
Of one single locomotive, straining at the week-by-week
Ever-steepening gradient of a hill of unsaleable ore.
The metals undulated bumpily over hillock and hollow
Like a fairground roller-coaster; screes of ore
Dustbinned on to rusty willows; the romanesque brick pit-head
Towers of Number Ten now and then twirled their wheels,
Lifting a couple of miners or half a ton of ore.
We scuffed through a scabbed and scruffy valley of ruddled rocks
To Cumberland's southernmost point, a headland, half-
    blasted-away,
Where the limestone met the tide. Here, on the seaward side,
Wave-action moulds the rocks, thumbs them like plasticine;
Landward the crag splits vertical down to the old workings.
We traversed the yard-wide col between quicksand and quarry,
    and there,
In a cockle-shell dip in the limestone, matted with thrift and
    rock-rose,
Was Sunday's flower, the Bloody Cranesbill,* red as the ore
It grew from, fragile as Venetian glass, pencilled with metal-
    thread
Haematite-purple veins. The frail cups lay so gently

On their small glazed saucer-bracts that a whisper would have
  tipped them over
Like emptying tea-leaves out. Every Sunday morning
I bent and picked one flower and every time it withered
Before we were half-way home to my Uncle Jim's. Fifty years
  later,
And it's hard to tell there ever was a mine: pit-heads
Demolished, pit-banks levelled, railway-lines ripped up,
Quarries choked and flooded, and all the lovely resistance
Of blackberry, blackthorn, heather and willow grubbed up and
  flattened.
A barren slack of clay is slurried and scaled-out over
All that living fracas of top-soil and rock. A town's
Purpose subsides with the mine; my father and my Uncle Jim
Lie a quarter of a century dead; but out on its stubborn skerry,
In a lagoon of despoliation, that same flower
                    Still grows today.

* The Bloody Cranesbill, *Geranium sanguineum*, is fairly common at a
number of places on the Cumbrian coast.

Comprehending It Not

December, 1921. Seven years of age,
And my mother dead—the house in mourning,
The shop shut up for Christmas—I
Was fobbed off to my Grandma's with my Christmas Tree
Bundled under my arm. Out
In the brown packed streets the lamplight drizzled down
On squirming pavements; the after-smell of war
Clung like a fungus to wall and window-sill,
And the backyards reeked of poverty. Boys,
Their big toes squirting through their boots,
Growled out *While Shepherds Watched* to deaf door-knobs,
And the Salvation Army—euphoniums, slung unplaying—
Stumped the length of the town at the thump of a drum
To cracked Hallelujahs in the Market Square.

I edged past muttering entries, sidled inside the lobby,
And slammed the door on the dark. My Grandma
Banged the floor with her stick to greet me,
Tossed me a humbug and turned again to the goose,
Spluttering on the kitchen range. My four rough uncles
Barged jokily around in flannel shirtsleeves,
Challenged to comic fisticuffs or gripped me
With a wrestler's grip and hyped me and cross-buttocked
In Cumberland-and-Westmorland style—till puffed, at last, and
    weary
Of horse-play and of me, they ripped my Christmas
Tree from its wrapper, unfolded its gaunt
Umbrella frame of branches, stuck candles in the green raffia,
And stood it on the dresser, well out of my reach.

I crouched down by the fire, crunching my humbug,
And scissoring holly and bells from coloured card;
The huff of the smoke brought water to my eyes,
The smell of the goose made me retch. Then suddenly,
The gas plopped out and the house was doused in darkness—

A break in the main and not a chance of repair
Till the day after Boxing Day. Matches rattled;
A twist of paper torn from the *Daily Mail*
Relayed the flame from grate to candle,
And soon, high on the dresser, my Christmas Tree,
Ignited like a gorse-bush, pollened the room with light.

Proud as a proselyte,
I stuffed white wax in the mouth of a medicine bottle,
Pioneered the wild lobby and the attic stairs
And dared the heathen flagstones of the yard,
Bearing my gleam of a gospel. At the scratch of a match,
Christmas crackled up between winter walls,
And Grandma's house was home, her sharp voice called in
    kindness,
And the fists no longer frightened. Tickled at the trick of it,
I 'Merry-Christmased' gas-pipe, gas and gas-men,
'God-blessed' the darkness and pulled crackers with the cold—
Scarcely aware what it was that I rejoiced in:
Whether the black-out or the candles,
Whether the light or the dark.

Halley's Comet

My father saw it back in 1910,
The year King Edward died.
Above dark telegraph poles, above the high
Spiked steeple of the Liberal Club, the white
Gas-lit dials of the Market Clock,
Beyond the wide
Sunset-glow cirrus of blast-furnace smoke,
My father saw it fly
Its thirty-seven-million-mile-long kite
Across Black Combe's black sky.

And what of me,
Born four years too late?
Will I have breath to wait
Till the long-circuiting commercial traveller
Turns up at his due?
In 1986, aged seventy-two,
Watery in the eyes and phlegmy in the flue
And a bit bad tempered at so delayed a date,
Will I look out above whatever is left of the town—
The Liberal Club long closed and the clock stopped,
And the chimneys smokeless above damped-down
Furnace fires? And then will I
At last have chance to see it
With my own as well as my father's eyes,
And share his long-ago Edwardian surprise
At that high, silent jet, laying its bright trail
Across Black Combe's black sky?